Native to Strange

Thomas Hanchett

I OPEN MY

I open my

eyes
under

water, and

all
I see

are these

words.

THE SPRINGTIME OF MY COMPLETELY

The springtime of my completely

here

is

reddening

into a swollen

something-or-other

I'll describe

later

in

more

language.

When it's gone,

happiness is

an abstracted

picnic in

May

beneath

an enormous

yew on the gentle sunny

side of a hill, with friends

and family, in the miracle

of their being

no difference

between the two.

A MILLION LEAVES

A million leaves
from quiet

a bird

can't

sing.

…

Terror in the home
grows a demon

lung

to breathe.

…

And every
eyelash
has

a name.

I FAITH

I faith

my

way

to finding
a dandelion,

with or without

a
home.

FOR THE FOX IN THE SNOW

It's the oldest

pop

song

in the heart's

rotation of greatest

hits: *she is my affliction*

only

she

can

cure.

I wasn't

planning to hear

this song again. I kept

repeating

the one

before it

about the flower

next to the river

that

bloomed

forever, because

it was stone. She

is my endlessness

beginning.

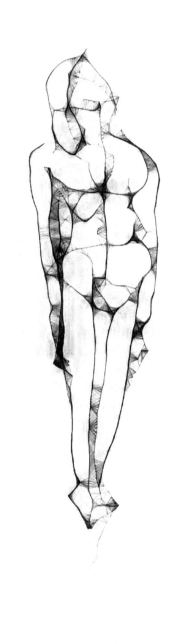

A MAN IN LOVE

A man in love
is an absurd

crocus.

I BREATHE SIMPLICITY

I breathe simplicity
in, because it
tastes

like
the thing
that nourishes

my root.

I breathe out
complexity

because
it nourishes

the sky.

I don't know why
this moon won't
wash

yesterday
into a translation

I can read, together.

…

You are unreachable

as the underground
invisibilities

you
worship.
…

And I don't mind
tomorrow or
feeling.

TAINTED BY THE SONG

Tainted by the song
and no longer
wary

of life
in all its

wrong
colors,

in all its scary

shapes,

I pause
and belong.

Tainted by the song
you sang about the cherry

chapstick during our

long
waking

in the strong
morning,

I will carry
everything

and be
merry.

Tainted by the song,
I'm no longer
wary.

CURRENTLY A WHITE

Currently a white

male

sort of

tingling with

guilt
and
ambition.

FAITH

In the middle
of a lake

of reasons
to stay

in the boat,
I went

swimming.

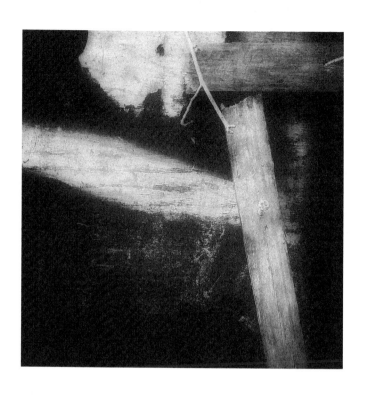

WHAT IF

What if
the adventure
was a gun against

your temple
of flirtation
with commitment?

…

Cold and happy
at last

in the rough
deprivation of

needing
to survive—

uncontrived.

Because for a moment
you were gone

into the fascination

of true
fear.

IT WAS DARK AND THE CEILING

It was dark and the ceiling

was low, as they climbed

through the interior

of St. Peter's. At the base of yet

another

stairway, he paused

to look out a small, casement

window

at the clear, blue, Roman sky.

His sister and brother-in-law

waited

a moment for him,

and then disappeared

into the higher

dark.

AFTER EASING MORE DIRT

After easing more dirt
into the crevices
around

the last brick

on the path

to her driveway,

she packed the dirt
down with the
butt

end of her spade,

then with her fingers.

She rose and stepped on

the brick, lightly at first, then

with all her weight. It wiggled

slightly, before

it was

still.

I AM GOING

I am going
to spell
this

out.

In the lee,
I am
safe.

…

How many tors
has it been,
since my

skin
was soft?

…

Late in the mountain
a river speaks
to the down

way
of the sore
hearted,

keep going.

WATER IN MY

Water in my
teacup

is astonished
with

flavor.

I GUARD YOUR SLEEP

I guard your sleep

because I am

alone

in

the garden

of momentary.

Our cat is crying

to be let in,

to be let

out,

to be fed, to be

loved, to

be solitary.

Like this poem.

I guard your sleep

because in the

clearing

of

your

dreams, I

imagine you

recovering the song

of your own

sacred

freedom.

HOW DO I STOP

How do I stop
the vivid

flower

of this letting
go?

A WORD AGAINST

A word against
the wind

devastating

our

mood:

she and I are kin, one
word
against

the wind.

I listen through
the din

to the shell
of her nude

pelvis

straining to win
poignancy from skin,

more urgently
than sin.

Deeper I go
in, where

no other
souls

intrude.

EVERY EXPRESSION

Every expression

on every

face

a fist

when I am sleep

deprived.

TOO LONG A CONVERSATION

Too long a conversation
with bright-eyed
silence

and
I am

smitten with fear
of losing
her.

APPARENTLY NOT ENTIRELY

Apparently not entirely

content

living

on

the

other

side of my

oblivion, happiness

surprised

me

nearby

in the guise

of joy, for several

hours.

I figured

goodbye was

the easiest gratitude

when the night

was twilight.

But

something is

changing

im

possible

to reasonable, to

yes. I can't explain

the difference, between this

and

pure

sunlight.

AS THEY EMBRACED, SHE

As they embraced, she
pressed her face into
the damp material
of his black

sweatshirt, and
felt

the fate
of her body

belonging.

It was late and they
were tired of skin,
so

they removed
everything

and began.

Afterward, he searched
in the darkness for her red
panties, so they could recover

from
the loss.

GOD, TELL ME

God, tell me

this

is real.

This being

here, among

the trees

the stones

the mist,

unforsaken

by the sun.

Ruined by a word

spoken

out

of tune,

I dance alone

to invisibilities

of chance

until

I am one.

She is the journey

I begin

to suspect

is

my

last.

Change

me

love,

into

myself.

HER DAUGHTER'S TINY

Her daughter's tiny
lips tickled
her

left
nipple.
…

When the baby
was finished
eating

they

took a nap
on the couch,

not

watching
the remainder

of *You Can Count on Me*,

the DVD her younger

brother had given

her

for Christmas,

that was still
playing

on
the flatscreen.

…

When she awoke,
it was already
dark.

BECAUSE I AM

Because I am
holy, as the wind

as the rain,

I will marry again
the certainty of
change.

As the wind in
the rain formulates
a mind,

the certainly of
change is a matter

of chance.

Formulate your
mind
toward
the needful

ground. In a matter
of chance, win
for the exception.

Out of needless
ground, tilting
in the sun,
one

of the exceptions,
an iris growing
wild.

Willing as the sun,
I shall marry
again

an iris,
bold and wild,

because she is wholly.

MY FEELING FOR HER

My feeling for her
skin

is

an

opalescent
din of remembering

how I am.

ONLY ANGELS

Only angels
know

how
to forget

the summertime.

…

A seagull narrates
the beginning of
evening

over
Pike Street
to the beguiled

few

in a flight
of happenstance.

I am
too

forgotten

past the letter

to listen

for
a middle.

…

Whimsy has a
special

name

for the ability
to remain

en
route

to nowhere.

…

Get behind me,
future.

I MISS YOU

I miss you,

baby,

said the mile

to the kilometer

inside

of

itself. *I'm right*

here,

said

the calmer

distance. Together was

insufficient for the

passion

of

this. Streets

regulate

direction of cars

and sidewalks,

pedestrians. So

no

wonder the fire

of the mind, catches

the heart

unaware

and

helpless. When

will

we

learn,

timely?

I WAS CONTENT

I was content

to live

under

ground. I'd

put away

my

eyes

and ears.

And then you

came

digging.

SPIDER ON THE BATHROOM

Spider on the bathroom
floor,

still
as a tangle

of knotted hair.

I KNOW NOTHING

I know nothing

and no

one

except

this page,

on a night

when the rain

cures

the ground

of its imagination.

I'M GIVING BACK

I'm giving back
the keys
to

the paradise of nought.
I'm rising from
my knees

and
giving
back the

keys.

At the bottom
of the sea's
a solitude

I sought. There I learned
to ease the amplitude
of *ought*,

and creatures
like the breeze
brushed against

my thought,
and

in

me
feelings
wrought. I swear

I don't need these
anymore. Take
back

the keys
to my paradigm

of nought.

WHERE DID WE GO WRONG

Where did we go wrong

pop

song?

You were so tired

in my arms

we

slept

forever,

it was milk

to my otherwise.

Now I prefer white noise
to your exclamations of

easy
sunlight

or easier

declarations

of eternal night.

I'm taking off the sweater
we bought together, and

feeling the air

of
what

essentially.

SHE WATCHED THE BEE

She watched the bee
land on the scalloped

edge of a daffodil,

and touch the surface

tastingly with vertical
dashes of fingerly

tongue.

Where in the poetry
of earth was there

a word for such a dulcet endeavor?

She opened her Watts
and traced the bee

with her pinky
finger

into

a line

of music.

NATURE IS ALONE

Nature is alone
in the bare
red

branches,
reaching of a tree

past the dead,
revival.

Winter

in her calm

finds a hawthorn

respite,

daring it

to
move.

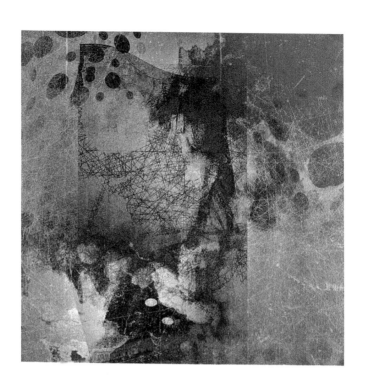

OLDER THAN SIN

Older than sin,
and just as
canny,

joy.

WHEN HER MIND WAS MADE UP

When her mind was made up,

she pressed E1 and

watched the

black

spiral

holding

the yellow

pack of peanut

M&Ms on the upper

middle row of the vending

machine, turn counter clockwise

to the decorous, tinny

tune of something

happening

because

of money.

When the music stopped

the candy hung, unfallen

and almost

hers.

YOU CAN STILL WALK

You can still walk
your old imagination

to Cal Anderson Park,
and watch it chase

forever

among the silver

grass, in the expiring
light of a December

afternoon, when
the world is

saved
by

what
remains.

…

The administrator
of greatness

sleeps
in the guest

room of humility

…

as we endeavor
to actually

smell

a lilac.

NOT BECAUSE I HAVE

Not because I have

to genuflect

to

shy

or calibrate my

blue; I sidle

up

to you

not because I

have

to

deviate from sky
or fantasize
a *why*.

I want

to go awry

with you, pretending

new. Can't we

be
untrue

to the edict

of goodbye?

I

mumble

in the pew,

not because I have to

genuflect; or

die.

KIND

Kind

of like

the sentimental

word unsaid,

lightning in a shiverstorm

body

withheld;

cry my hand

to underneath

your wild measure.

Savor me

as

sleep.

ADJACENT TO WHATEVER

Adjacent to whatever

mood

your

momentary

calls

home,

is a circumstance

of perfectly

awake.

She can taste your seeing

her hearing you feel

how near

she appreciates your

scent. It was always

this

real, and you knew

it. Which is why

you

understood

the morning.

The seagull's cry

is the joyful

abstraction

of a sunrise.

INSTEAD OF SAYING THE WORDS

Instead of saying the words

that were glowing in

a pyrotechnical

font

across

the undifferentiated

landscape and sky of her

heart and mind, she

kissed the man

beneath her

on the neck, and

then the chest, and

then the stomach; before

he

pulled

her back

to the scarier

intimacy of saying

the burning

words,

first.

I AM A MURDERER

I am a murderer

of formerly

no.

It took
planning

and
ingenuity

and opportunity.

Now I grow and grow
into the nothing
and the

silence,

where the first purple
crocus bleeds out

of
snow.

Imprint

Thomas Hanchett · Native to Strange

September 2016

© Poems & Cover Photo
Thomas Hanchett · torleeword@gmail.com

© Paintings & Drawings
Corey Jay Sautter · corey_sautter@yahoo.com
instagram: @limbox7

© Verlag Alessandra Nobilia
Klappergasse 6 · 55270 Essenheim · Germany
nobilia-verlag.de · alessandra@nobilia-verlag.de

Printed by blurb.com

ISBN 978-3-9818243-1-5

CPSIA information can be obtained
at www.ICGtesting.com
Printed in the USA
FSOW04n0724110916
24871FS